Alexander Graham Bell and the Telephone

CORNERSTONES OF FREEDOM

SECOND SERIES

Christine Webster

Children's Press®
A Division of Scholastic Inc.
New York • Toronto • London • Auckland • Sydney
Mexico City • New Delhi • Hong Kong
Danbury, Connecticut

Photographs ©2004: Corbis Images: 33, cover top, 16, 21, 23, 30, 39, 44 center, 45 bottom (Bettmann), cover bottom (Minnesota Historical Society), 34 (Underwood & Underwood), 24; Hulton|Archive/Getty Images: 8, 13, 31, 32; Library of Congress: 4, 5, 6, 7, 9, 10 right, 10 left, 11, 12, 15, 17, 18 top, 20 right, 35, 36, 37, 38, 41, 44 top left, 45 top; North Wind Picture Archives: 18 bottom, 28, 29; Photo Researchers, NY: 22, 44 bottom (J-L Charmet/SPL), 3 (Library of Congress), 25 (Marten/Library of Congress), 26 (Seila Terry/SPL); Photos courtesy of SBC Archives and History Center, San Antonio, Texas: 19, 20 left, 44 top right.

Library of Congress Cataloging-in-Publication Data
Webster, Christine.
  Alexander Graham Bell and the telephone / Christine Webster.
     p. cm. — (Cornerstones of freedom. Second series)
Summary: Discusses the life and work of Alexander Graham Bell, focusing on his invention of the telephone.
  Includes bibliographical references and index.
    ISBN 0-516-24227-X
    1. Bell, Alexander Graham, 1847–1922—Juvenile literature.
2. Inventors—United States—Biography—Juvenile literature.
3. Telephone—History—Juvenile literature. [1. Bell, Alexander Graham, 1847–1922. 2. Inventors.] I. Title. II. Series.
TK6143.B4W45 2003
621.385'092—dc21

                                              2003011243

1 2 3 4 5 6 7 8 9 10 R 13 12 11 10 09 08 07 06 05 04

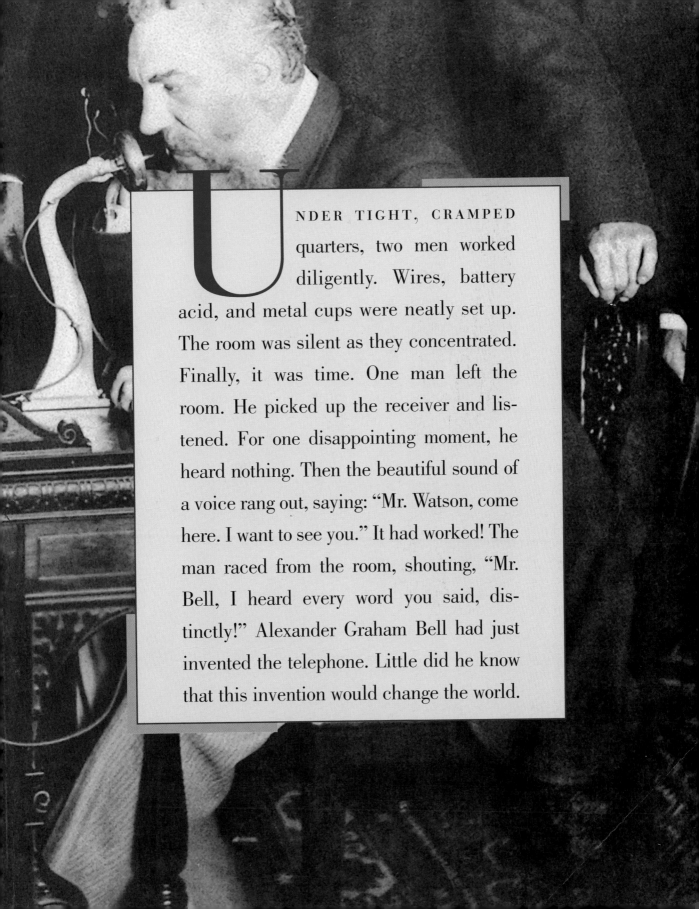

UNDER TIGHT, CRAMPED quarters, two men worked diligently. Wires, battery acid, and metal cups were neatly set up. The room was silent as they concentrated. Finally, it was time. One man left the room. He picked up the receiver and listened. For one disappointing moment, he heard nothing. Then the beautiful sound of a voice rang out, saying: "Mr. Watson, come here. I want to see you." It had worked! The man raced from the room, shouting, "Mr. Bell, I heard every word you said, distinctly!" Alexander Graham Bell had just invented the telephone. Little did he know that this invention would change the world.

Bell (above) and his mother, Eliza (right), shared a love of music. Eliza Bell is shown on a velocipede, a type of old-fashioned bicycle.

* * * *

FAMILY TIES

In the mid-1800s, Edinburgh, Scotland, was brimming with scientific and technological advancements and discoveries. Streets were powered by gas lamps, railroads were spreading across the country, and the electric **telegraph** had arrived with the ability to send almost-instant messages. From these advancements, even more ideas would bloom.

Alexander Graham Bell was born in Edinburgh on March 3, 1847. He was the middle child, between elder brother Melville and younger brother Edward. From the day he was born, Bell's life was shaped by sound. Although his mother, Eliza Grace Bell, was **hearing impaired**, she taught him to

play the piano. He was a very good piano player and had a remarkable ear for tones and sounds. Bell also developed an interest in speech, thanks to his father and his grandfather. His grandfather, Alexander, and his father, Alexander Melville, believed that people should strive for the finest communication. Originally a Scottish shoemaker and actor, Alexander Bell opened a school in London to teach the art of public speaking, known as **elocution**. He often used the elegant Shakespearean language he had studied during his brief acting career as a guideline for his classes.

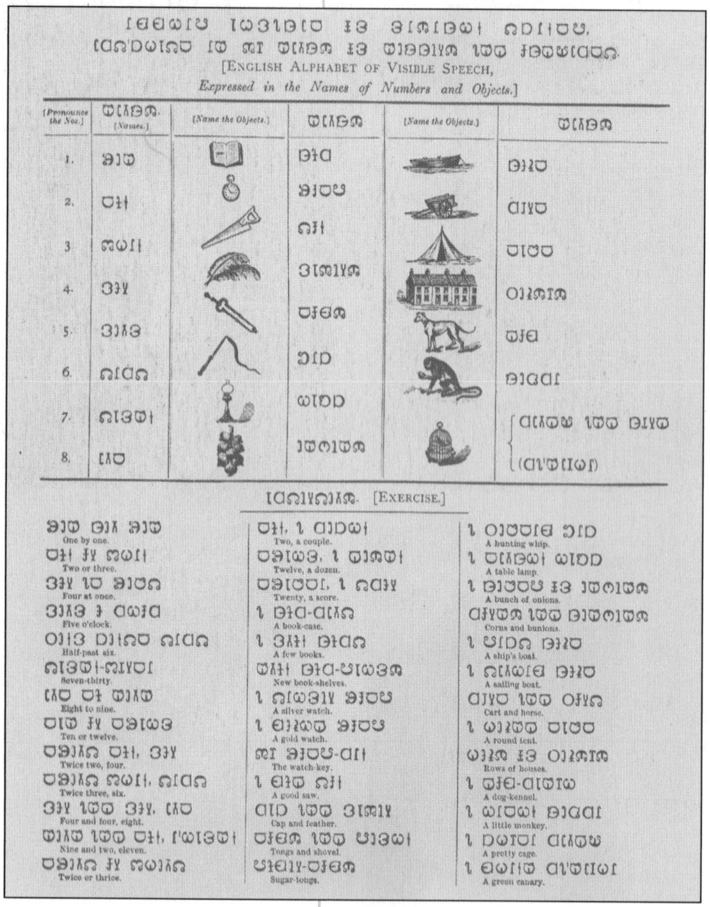

Bell's father, Melville, was also involved in the school. Melville Bell studied sound at two local universities. He later invented a system called Visible Speech that consisted of a group of thirty-four symbols. These symbols described or represented the sounds that we make when we talk. The symbols showed the position of the tongue, the teeth, the throat, and the lips when a particular sound is made. The Visible Speech system could train any person to reproduce any sound made by humans—including coughs, clicks, and sneezes. Melville Bell used the

The symbols of Visible Speech, shown below, could be used to represent any sound that could be made by the human mouth.

[ENGLISH ALPHABET OF VISIBLE SPEECH, Expressed in the Names of Numbers and Objects.]

system to teach people to **enunciate**, or speak properly. He also used it to help people with speech problems such as stammering.

After learning about his father's Visible Speech system, Bell thought that it could also be used to teach hearing-impaired people to speak. Those who are born hearing impaired are unable to learn speech because they cannot hear how sounds are produced. Each of these symbols represented a specific way that a person uses his or her lips, tongue, or throat to produce a sound, so a student could make any sound just by reading a page of symbols. The hearing impaired could learn to communicate without using sign language.

Bell and his older brother often helped their father to demonstrate the system to the public. During some lectures, the brothers left the room while the audience suggested words that their father wrote as symbols on a chalkboard. When the boys returned and read the symbols, they were always able to correctly identify the words. Over the years, Bell and his older brother astounded audiences, who often tried to trick the two but were not successful.

Alexander Melville Bell, shown here with his son, was an authority on elocution, the art of speaking clearly and correctly. He encouraged Bell to be a more serious student.

7

This illustration shows a busy street in London around 1850. Bell's grandfather, Alexander Bell, made a name for himself there by giving lessons in speech and elocution.

A MIDDLE NAME

Bell didn't have a middle name until he was eleven years old, when a family friend named Alexander Graham came to visit. Bell liked the way the two names sounded, and from then on he began using the name Alexander Graham Bell.

SCIENTIFIC CURIOSITY

When Bell was about fifteen years old, he went to London to study with his grandfather. Alexander had a great influence on his grandson. It was during this year that Bell decided what he wanted to do in life. Like his father and his grandfather, he, too, wanted to study speech, as well as sound.

When Bell returned home from London, he and his brothers began experimenting with sounds. One such experiment involved a model of a human vocal

apparatus. The model contained all the necessary ingredients needed to create sound, including a head, a mouth, a tongue, a throat, a windpipe, and lungs. Blowing through the model produced a loud bellow, which sounded like a baby crying "Mama!" This confused the neighbors, who knew that the Bells did not have a baby.

Another remarkable experiment also caused quite a stir. Bell used the family dog for an experiment that actually made the terrier speak English. He discovered that, by moving the dog's mouth and throat with his hands, he could produce sounds from the dog that resembled words. With Bell's help, the terrier was able to say "Ow ah oo, ga-ma-ma?" This translated into "How are you, grandmother?" Imagine his parents' surprise at their talking terrier!

At the age of sixteen, Bell left home once again, to teach and study. In return for his teaching of elocution and music, a boys' school in northern Scotland provided him with free studies. During his studies at Weston House, he read about experiments by a German scientist named Hermann von Helmholtz. In the book, the scientist described how he was able to reproduce **artificial** vowel sounds by

As a teenager, Bell and his brother began to experiment with sound.

9

using tuning forks and electricity. A tuning fork is a metal instrument that consists of two **prongs**, similar to a dinner fork. When the tuning fork is struck, it vibrates and produces a tone or sound.

Fortunately for today's modern world, Bell didn't fully understand this book. He thought that the scientist was actually sending vowel sounds through an electric wire. Because of this misunderstanding, Bell turned his thoughts to sending sound over distance by using electricity. He wanted to find a way to telegraph sounds. These thoughts would eventually lead him to the telephone.

ONWARD TO CANADA

In 1867, while Bell was away at college, he was suddenly called home. Tragedy had struck the Bell family. His younger brother, Edward, had died of tuberculosis, a disease of the lungs. Bell rushed home to be by his family's side.

Both Edward (left) and Melville (right) died of tuberculosis—an infectious disease that usually attacks the lungs.

Alexander recovered from his illness at this house in Ontario, Canada.

He stayed in London during the next few years, helping his father with Visible Speech and studying at the University of London. Three years later, tragedy struck his family once again. His elder brother, Melville, also succumbed to tuberculosis. Grief-stricken and exhausted, Bell himself became ill, and his parents panicked. They knew they had to do something to save their only surviving son. Bell's father thought that the air in Canada would be fresher and cleaner due to its cooler climate. The fresh, smog-free air would help him breathe better. To save their son's life, the Bell family packed up and headed to Ontario, Canada.

After fourteen days traveling across the Atlantic Ocean, the Bells settled on a farm near Brantford in southern Ontario. His parents had done the right thing. Gradually, their twenty-three-year-old son's health improved, and he was strong once again.

Bell posed for this picture dressed in traditional Mohawk clothing. His cousin, Frances Symonds, is seated at left.

THE MOHAWKS

While in Canada, Bell made friends with some neighboring Native Americans, the Mohawks. He learned to speak their language, and he recorded it in his father's Visible Speech system. In return, the Native Americans made him an honorary Mohawk and taught him their war dance. This privilege also allowed Bell to wear traditional Mohawk clothing.

* * * *

A NEW IDEA

Through the early 1800s, the telegraph was the main means of long-distance communication. The telegraph relied on a dot-and-dash method, relaying one message at a time over a wire using **Morse code**. The sender tapped out a message in code that was sent using an electric current traveling over a wire. At the other end, the electric current provided power to a machine for the receiver. The receiver could listen to the sounds, or a pointing machine would make dots on a sheet that the receiver could then decode. The message was then given to a messenger who would hand-deliver it to the intended recipient.

Two young women operate a Morse code machine at a receiving station, around 1888.

Bell, who continued to be fascinated by sound, knew that a telegraph capable of sending more than one message at a time would greatly benefit society. He began to think of ways to improve the telegraph. Although the idea of a multiple telegraph was not new, Bell took a unique approach. He used his musical experience to try to come up with a solution, figuring that several messages could be sent along one wire at the same time if the messages or signals were different from one another or had different tones. He often used his piano as a key subject in his studies because he had a keen ear for tones. By pressing one key on the piano and listening closely to the tone, he tried to analyze the sound. He continued for many years to think of ways to create his multiple telegraph. Through his experiments, the idea of human voice transmission was opened.

TEACHER OF THE HEARING IMPAIRED

In 1871, Bell was offered a job in Boston teaching hearing impaired children how to speak using the Visible Speech system. Although his father was originally requested for the job, he was too busy to accept the position. He suggested that his son go instead, because Bell understood the system and knew it well. In March 1871, at age twenty-four, Bell headed to the United States.

During the day, he taught at the Boston School for Deaf Mutes. At night, he experimented. His hopes of inventing a multiple telegraph were still high, but the experiments were

This photograph shows a group of students at the Boston School for Deaf Mutes, where Bell was a teacher.

expensive. To raise money, he began giving private lessons for the hearing impaired and their teachers in his home.

Bell was a dedicated teacher. He hated the thought of hearing-impaired children feeling isolated and alone. One way he helped his students was by creating a device called a phonautograph. It was used to help make sound visible to his students. Sound waves are movements or vibrations.

Bell began giving instruction in Visible Speech at a school in Boston.

When a sound is made, the vibrations travel through the air, similar to wind. The sound waves then carry the sound to the ear. The ear captures the sound and changes the vibrations into electric currents. These electric currents travel farther into the ear until they meet nerves that carry the sound information to the brain to determine what the sound is.

To demonstrate this process, Bell borrowed a human ear from a nearby medical school. He placed the ear at the narrow end of a tube; he then attached a stalk of hay to the middle-ear bones and put a glass plate on the other side of the hay. When a student spoke into the phonautograph, the sounds from his or her voice vibrated. These vibrations caused the hay to move, etching, or scratching, the pattern of the voice onto a plate of glass. This allowed the students to "see" their speech. By seeing it, Bell hoped they would be able to improve their speech.

THE BUSINESS OF INVENTION

In 1872, Bell became professor of vocal physiology and mechanics of speech at Boston University. As a result, he was able to meet and talk with many scientists about electricity and sound. Bell's students put him in contact with many businessmen, allowing Bell the opportunity to meet financial backers, or people who could

This is an advertisement for Bell's services as a professor.

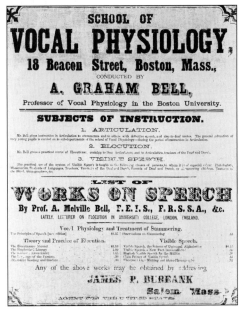

help pay for the cost of his experiments. Two of these businessmen were Gardiner Greene Hubbard and Thomas Sanders.

Hubbard was a Boston attorney. His daughter, Mabel, had suffered a serious bout of scarlet fever at age four that left her hearing impaired. When Mabel turned fifteen, Hubbard brought her to Bell for help. Bell and Mabel became quite fond of one another. Their relationship blossomed, and she would later become his wife.

Over time, Hubbard learned that Bell was trying to improve the telegraph. Hubbard, who often criticized the Western Union Telegraph Company for having too much control of the telegraph market, readily agreed to support Bell's experiments. He was hoping to outdo Western Union.

The Western Union Telegraph Company built the nation's first transcontinental (coast-to-coast) telegraph line. Western Union quickly became the largest company in its field.

Thomas Sanders was another wealthy man who became interested in Bell's experiment. His son, George, came to Bell as a student at the age of five. George quickly picked up on Bell's speech technique. Grateful to Bell, Sanders later agreed to contribute money to the multiple-telegraph experiments. Both Hubbard and Sanders were confident that they would later share in the profits of the invention when it was sold.

Bell soon began to realize that he lacked the time and skill to make all the necessary parts for his experiments. Hubbard insisted that Bell get help from someone who knew how to make electrical instruments. One such man was Thomas A. Watson. The twenty-year-old had an in-depth knowledge of electricity and experience working for inventors. He also worked in a shop that made electrical instruments. In January 1875, Bell hired Watson to help him build a model of the multiple telegraph. The two became fast friends.

Thomas Sanders helped finance Bell's multiple telegraph experiments.

THEY'VE DONE IT!

Bell and Watson worked hard each night on the multiple telegraph. Many other inventors were pursuing the same project, which added a sense of urgency to Bell and Watson's work. They spent long hours in the hot and stuffy

Thomas Watson worked closely with Bell to develop the telephone.

attic of the electric shop where Watson worked. They used many items in their experiments, such as tuning forks, wires, and batteries.

In spite of their efforts, Bell and Watson could not separate the sounds that were sent across the telegraph wires. Out of frustration, Bell told his assistant about another idea: carrying words rather than dots and dashes over an electric wire. Watson loved the concept—which would become known as the telephone—and thought they should pursue it. The two men decided to focus on the telephone as well as the multiple telegraph.

SPEAKING GREEK

The word *telephone* is made from two Greek words. *Tele* means "far off," and *phone* means "sound." So *telephone* means "far-off sound."

Bell and Watson rented the attic room of this building in downtown Boston to work on their experiments.

Bell and Watson worked long days and nights without results, until they made a breakthrough in June 1875.

Bell knew that to finish his invention he needed to take some time off from his other work, so he took a break from teaching and spent his days and nights experimenting. The extra time paid off. On June 2, 1875, Bell and Watson had a breakthrough.

It began when they replaced the tuning forks with metal **reeds**. The reeds produced sounds that vibrated longer and could be tuned better. In one room, Watson would make the reed on a **transmitter** vibrate. In a separate room, Bell would receive the sounds. Fortunately for the two inventors,

★ ★ ★ ★

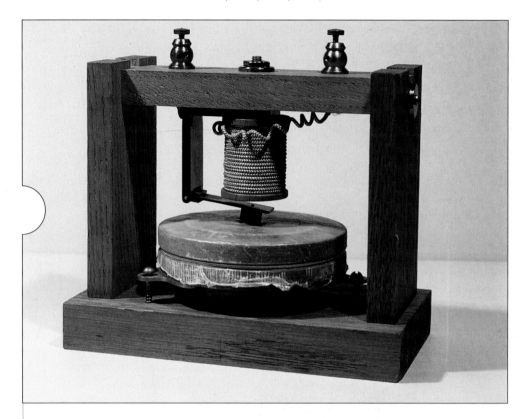

one of the reeds got stuck. Watson went to work trying to
free the reed by flicking it with his finger.

In another room, Bell heard a sound from the transmitter—*ping*. He couldn't believe his ears. For the first time,
sound was transmitted through electricity. After hearing this
sound through the wire, Bell and Watson knew it would be
possible to have speech go through the wire.

Confident, Watson began building a model of their telephone. The two men became obsessed with perfecting their
invention. Long days and nights were spent experimenting.
Voices were heard over the wire, but they could not be
understood. Still, they were making progress.

Bell felt it was now time to secure, or protect, his invention, so he began to write down details for a patent application. A patent is an official document issued by the government that gives only the inventor the right to make, use, or sell his or her invention for a certain amount of time. On Bell's behalf, Hubbard traveled to the patent office in Washington, D.C., to apply for a patent on February 14, 1876.

A FEW HOURS TOO LATE

Another man, Elisha Gray, (left) applied for a similar patent on the same day—just a few hours after Hubbard. At the time, Bell's patent claim stated that he had *already* invented the device, while Elisha Gray's claim stated only that he was *in the process of* inventing it. This made Bell the official owner of the telephone patent. Gray filed many lawsuits through the years, challenging Bell as the rightful owner of the telephone patent. It took eighteen years to prove that Bell was the original inventor.

In this photograph, taken around 1887, Bell and Watson examine their invention.

Just three days after Bell received his patent, on March 7, 1876, the inventors had another breakthrough. They began using a liquid-type transmitter to try to produce clearer sounds from the telephone. In this experiment they used wire, a metal cup, a metal needle, water, battery acid, a diaphragm (a flexible, or movable, membrane made of thin parchment, or paper), and a battery. Water and battery acid were mixed together in the metal cup, and a metal needle was placed in the liquid. One wire was used to connect the metal needle and a battery. The other wire was used to connect the battery with the metal cup, creating an electric circuit. The diaphragm was then placed in the metal cup. The two men were hopeful that this would work.

In a separate room, Watson put the receiver to his ear and listened. He couldn't believe what happened next. Although they were in separate rooms, Watson heard Bell's voice loud and clear through the receiver: "Mr. Watson, come here. I want to see you." Watson rushed out of the room in amazement and shouted, "Mr. Bell, I heard every word you said, distinctly!"

How did this experiment work? When Bell spoke into the diaphragm it vibrated. This vibration then caused the metal needle to bob up and down in the liquid mixture. As the

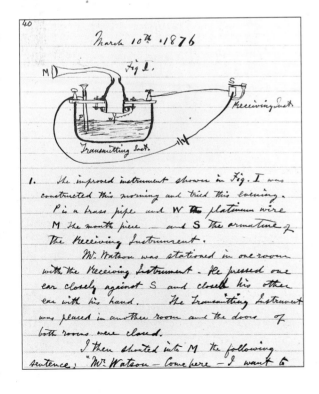

This page from Bell's notebook describes the experiments in detail.

A TIME TO DANCE

Although it is a matter of some dispute, it is thought that during the experiment Bell accidentally spilled battery acid on his pants. He was said to be so excited about their discovery that he ignored the mess and celebrated by doing his Mohawk war dance.

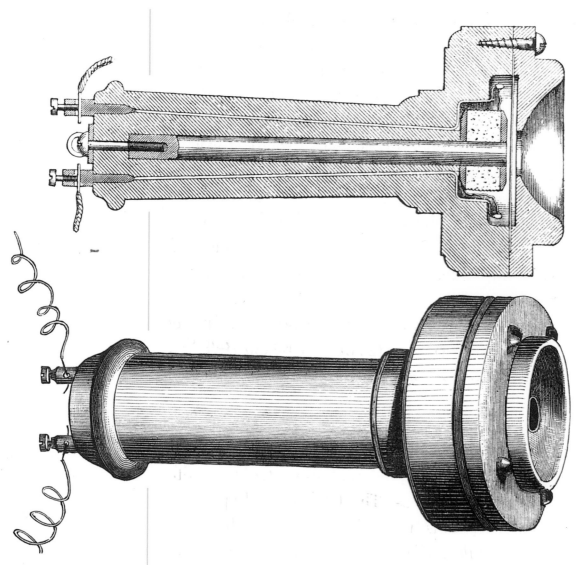

This historical artwork shows the inner workings of a Bell telephone.

needle moved up and down near the bottom of the cup, there was less resistance in the circuit. This caused the current to grow stronger. When the needle was moved away from the cup, the resistance increased, causing the current to become weaker.

The telephone receiver consisted of an **electromagnet** and a metal plate. An electromagnet is a powerful magnet made from coiling wire around an iron core many times and then sending an electric current through it. The telephone receiver imitated the sounds according to the shifting current. As the electromagnet grew stronger and weaker with the changing current, it pushed and pulled the metal plate. This caused the metal plate to vibrate and therefore imitate speech sounds, like the words Bell had said to Watson. The telephone receiver converted the electrical impulses back into recognizable sounds so that the words could be heard.

Although it was complicated, the experiment finally worked. At age twenty-nine, Alexander Graham Bell had sent the first telephone message in the world over a wire.

TESTING THE TELEPHONE

In June 1876, Bell took his new telephone to the Centennial Exposition in Philadelphia, a celebration of the hundredth birthday of the United States. The Centennial Exposition displayed great inventions from scientists around the country. One of these would be Bell's telephone, which he would publicly demonstrate to a panel of judges.

At the show, Bell watched as judges walked around the large room. No one seemed interested in his telephone. Just as the judges were about to leave for the day, a man recognized Bell. His name was Dom Pedro, the emperor of Brazil and the exhibition's guest of honor. Pedro, who remembered being

The Centennial Exposition celebrated 100 years of American progress. Of all the buildings at the fair, Machinery Hall—which displayed Bell's telephone, among other things—attracted the most attention.

impressed by Bell's teaching method for deaf students, insisted that his group have a look at Bell's invention.

Bell crossed the large room to sit with his transmitter. On the other side, Dom Pedro's party handled the receiver. Within moments, they were stunned to hear Bell's voice booming through the receiver reciting Shakespeare. Shocked, the

emperor of Brazil jumped from his chair exclaiming, "I hear, I hear!" The judges were impressed and awarded Bell a prize for his invention.

Although the exhibition had been a success, Bell wanted to test the telephone at greater distances. What good was an invention that could be used only by people in the same house?

This photograph shows Bell speaking into the Centennial telephone.

In the summer of 1876, during his vacation at home in Brantford, Ontario, Bell put the telephone to a number of tests. First he traveled about 5 miles (8 kilometers) from his home. On August 3, 1876, Bell set up his telephone in a telegraph office in a town called Mount Pleasant, just south of Brantford. From a Brantford telegraph office, he received a telephone call. Almost immediately he heard voices on the line. Although faint and unclear, the phone was working. The first test was a success.

Each time Bell tested the phone, he traveled farther away. He requested permission from the Dominion Telegraph Company to use its telegraph line between two Ontario towns, Brantford and Paris—a distance of 8 miles (13 km). With the company's approval, Bell set up his receiver in the Paris office. Many onlookers huddled in the room to find out if the telephone would work. Anxious and nervous, Bell listened closely. At first he couldn't hear much, and he wondered what was wrong. Using the telegraph, he sent a **telegram** telling those in the Brantford office to adjust the transmitter there. Almost instantly, harmonious voices sang through the phone.

SINGING FOR HOURS

Bell was given permission to use the Dominion Telegraph Company line for only one hour. With the excitement of the call, however, the people from Brantford continued to sing on the telephone for three hours, forgetting the one-hour time limit.

Bell began to test his invention over long distances.

TELEPHONE POPULARITY

Bell's invention caught on quickly as he gave lectures and demonstrations to people throughout the northeastern United States. The world's first outdoor telephone wire was set up in 1877. By May of that year the first telephone was rented for personal use. A young banker rented telephones for his home and his business so that he could communicate between the two places. Bell was quickly becoming famous; so was the telephone.

Advertisements for the telephone were prepared to promote it; however, they also advised caution. The ads stated that the telephone could carry a conversation over distances

Bell demonstrated his telephone in front of a crowd at Lyceum Hall in Salem, Massachusetts.

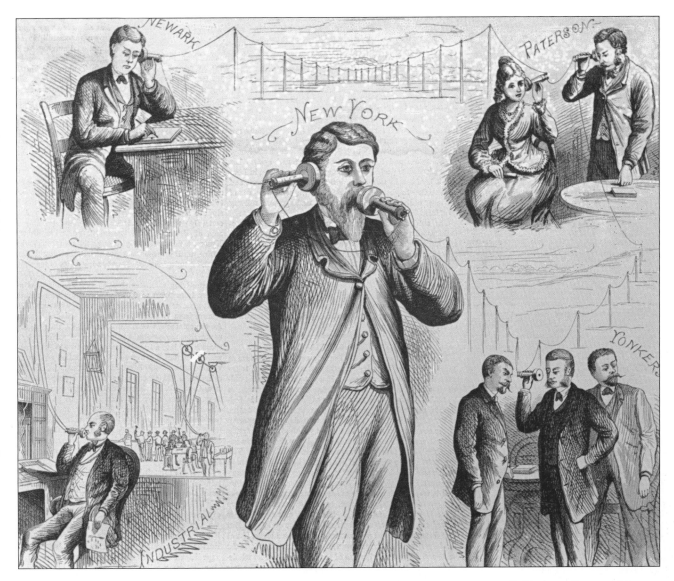

Bell's invention caught on quickly. This 1877 woodcut shows early applications of the Bell telephone.

of about 20 miles (32 km) but needed constant repetition of words or sentences and had a peculiar sound.

By July 1877, the first telephone company was created. On July 9, 1877, the Bell Telephone Company came into existence. Bell, Watson, Hubbard, and Sanders were partners. Two days later, Alexander Graham Bell married his

It wasn't long before switchboards were introduced. A switchboard allowed people on one phone line to be connected to those on another line. This photograph shows a Bell Atlantic switchboard operator at work in the 1930s.

sweetheart, Mabel Hubbard. As a wedding gift, Alexander gave his wife most of his shares in the newly formed company. The two honeymooned in England and continued to promote the telephone.

While in England, Bell had an opportunity to demonstrate his telephone to the Queen of England. Although **etiquette** forbade him from touching royalty, Bell placed his hand on Queen Victoria's to help her hold the receiver properly during a demonstration. Fortunately, she was too excited to notice. The queen was so impressed that she wanted to buy the two telephones that he used for the demonstration. She eventually had one of the first telephones in England installed at Windsor Castle.

In May 1878, while staying at a rented house in London, Mabel gave birth to their first child, a daughter they named Elsie. By this time, Bell was becoming bored of the telephone. After months of lecturing and demonstrations, he wanted to move on. Now wealthy, Bell looked to the future. He knew he was not a businessman. He was an inventor and was anxious to discover new things. In 1880, Bell left the business to his partners so he could pursue his love of inventing.

WEDDED TO INVENTION

In 1876, a disagreement between Bell and Mabel's father, Gardiner Greene Hubbard, almost prevented Bell's wedding. Hubbard became angry that Bell was spending all his time on the telephone, and neglecting the original invention that Hubbard had invested in, the multiple telegraph. Hubbard asked his daughter to refuse to marry Bell unless he devoted his time to this invention. As a result of several heated arguments, Bell agreed to continue work on the multiple telegraph as well as the telephone. Eventually Hubbard agreed that the telephone was a worthwhile invention.

Mabel holds daughter Elsie, born in 1878.

This Bell family portrait was taken in 1885.

THE FINAL YEARS

In 1879, the Bells moved to Washington, D.C. Mabel gave birth to their second daughter, Marian, in 1880. Bell continued to invent, receiving awards and honors from universities and scientific societies. The country of France awarded him the prestigious Volta Prize for his invention of the telephone.

Bell founded a school for the deaf on the second floor of this building in Washington, D.C.

The prize was worth so much money it allowed Bell to open a laboratory in Washington, D.C. This laboratory would enable Bell and other inventors to discover, invent, and bring new ideas to life.

Although several of his inventions proved prosperous, Alexander Graham Bell's work for the hearing impaired never ceased. He later founded a school for the hearing impaired in Washington, D.C. Bell also fought for the rights of hearing-impaired children. He hoped to give all hearing-impaired children the chance to speak.

37

THE GIFT OF SPEECH

When Bell began working with the hearing impaired, forty percent of hearing-impaired children were taught to speak using the Visible Speech system. By the time of his death, more than eighty percent of children who were hearing impaired were able to speak.

Bell and his wife spent summers at Beinn Bhreagh estate in Nova Scotia. He continued to invent while at the estate.

When he wasn't advocating for the rights of the hearing impaired, Bell enjoyed spending time in Canada. He built a beautiful family home on Cape Breton Island in Nova Scotia. Every summer he and Mabel took their two daughters to spend vacations in the village that reminded him of Scotland. They called their home Beinn Bhreagh, which means "beautiful mountain" in Gaelic. Although Bell had a laboratory built for his inventions, the family also relaxed there.

Bell dedicated his life to invention and discovery. He is shown here exhibiting a giant kite, or flying machine, around 1904.

The Bells returned to their summer retreat each year for almost forty years.

By 1915, the first transcontinental phone line was ready. From New York, Bell telephoned his dear friend Watson in San Francisco—almost 3,000 miles (4,828 km) away. When Watson answered the call he heard

A SCIENTIFIC INTERRUPTION

Ironically, Bell found the telephone to be somewhat disruptive. Although he had a telephone in his home, he refused to have one in his study.

the familiar and now-famous words, "Mr. Watson, come here. I want to see you." Watson jokingly replied, "But it will take me a week to reach you now!"

Throughout Bell's lifetime he was awarded more than twenty medals and twelve honorary degrees. He continued to invent many things. His medical inventions included a vacuum jacket that would help a person breathe and a device that detected bullets in the human body in order to better remove them. The bullet detector became very useful in later years, especially during World War I. Other items he invented included a photophone (something that transmits speech without wire), a **tetrahedral** kite (in the shape of a triangle, with four faces), and an audiometer (a device to test hearing).

Sadly, on August 2, 1922, Bell ceased inventing. Holding his beloved wife's hand, Alexander Graham Bell passed away at the age of seventy-five. In respect for the man who invented the telephone and changed the world forever, all telephones (about 13 million) throughout North America were kept silent for one minute.

Although Bell died many years ago, we are reminded of this great inventor every time we pick up the telephone. The world continues to invent, but nothing can ever replace the personal sound of a loved one's voice. Alexander Graham Bell may have once been bored of his invention, but our modern-day world will never tire of it.

A WORLD CONNECTED

In the first month that telephones were available, only six were sold. Today, it is estimated that there are more than five hundred million telephones around the world. They require more than 149,084,370 telephone lines. Thousands more are added every day.

Bell's invention changed the world and its limitations. In the words of Thomas Edison, the telephone "brought the human family closer in touch."

Glossary

apparatus—tools, equipment, or machinery used for a certain activity

artificial—something that is made by humans and is not natural

electromagnet—a powerful magnet made by coiling wire many times around an iron core and sending an electric current through it

elocution—the art of public speaking

enunciate—to speak or pronounce words clearly

etiquette—a specific way to conduct oneself in public

hearing impaired—unable to hear well or at all

larynx—the part of the throat that contains the vocal cords

Morse code—a signaling system that uses dots and dashes or long and short sounds to stand for letters and numbers

prongs—pointed ends of a fork, rake, or other instrument

reeds—thin slices of stalk or metal used to make sound when air moves through them

telegram—a message sent by special signals over wires from one area to another, then written down and delivered by hand

telegraph—the system of sending and receiving telegrams

tetrahedral—of or relating to a solid figure with four triangular faces

transmitter—a device that sends out signals carrying sounds

Timeline: Alexander Graham

1847	1870	1871	1872	1875	1876	1877

Alexander Graham Bell is born on March 3 in Edinburgh, Scotland.

The Bell family moves to Canada to save their only surviving son from tuberculosis.

Bell begins teaching in Boston at a school for the deaf.

Bell begins giving private lessons to teachers of the deaf.

Bell hires Thomas A. Watson as his assistant to help him design the multiple telegraph.

A patent for the telephone is issued to Bell.

The first telephone call in the world is received.

The Bell Telephone Company is formed.

Mabel and Bell are married.

Bell and the Telephone

1878 1880 1880 1883 1895 1897 1915

1878 — Mabel gives birth to their first child, Elsie May.

1880 — Bell receives a $10,000 prize from France called the Volta Prize.

1880 — A second child, Marian (Daisy), is born to the Bells.

1883 — Bell opens a school for the hearing impaired in Washington, D.C.

1895 — Bell begins experimenting with flight and planes.

1897 — Bell becomes president of the National Geographic Society.

1915 — The first transcontinental phone line opens.

1922 1923

1922 — Alexander Graham Bell dies on August 2 at his Canadian home, Beinn Bhreagh.

1923 — Mabel Hubbard Bell passes away.

To Find Out More

BOOKS AND JOURNALS

Durrett, Deanne. *Alexander Graham Bell*. San Diego, Calif.: KidHaven Press, 2002.

Ford, T. Carin. *Alexander Graham Bell: Inventor of the Telephone*. Berkeley Heights, NJ: Enslow Publishers, 2002.

McCormick, Anita Louise. *The Invention of the Telegraph and Telephone in American History*. Berkeley Heights, NJ: Enslow Publishers, 2004.

ONLINE SITES

Alexander Graham Bell Family Collection
http://bell.uccb.ns.ca/kidsindex.asp

Inventing the Telephone: AT&T History
http://www.att.com/history/inventing.html

AT&T Labs—For Fun
http://www.att.com/attlabs/technology/forfun/alexbell/

Index

Bold numbers indicate illustrations.

About the Author

Christine Webster is a children's author with a special interest in United States and Canadian history. Her work for Children's Press includes books in the From Sea to Shining Sea series and the Cornerstones of Freedom series, including *The Lewis and Clark Expedition* and *The Pledge of Allegiance*. She lives in Canada with her husband and four children.